MONET'S
Gardens

Catherine de Duve

For trainee painters and budding gardeners

KATE'ART
EDITIONS

Hello, my name is Claude Monet. I love gardening and painting my garden.

What a lovely colour! These purple irises painted 'from nature' make my prickles tingle!

Claude Monet lives in a pink house with green shutters in the village of Giverny, in Normandy.

Every day, the painter gets up with the sun and admires his garden. He also goes to bed when the sun goes down.

zzz...

Once the sun has gone, what can Claude Monet do?

"My studio? It's my garden, of course!"

Artists usually paint in their studio, but Monet paints in his garden. His canvas is taller than he is! So how can he paint on it? Monet takes his spade and digs a trench in the ground. With a pulley, he lowers the canvas into the trench.

What is he going to paint? A landscape and four ladies in dresses with crinolines. The sun is shining. The dresses are bright white in the sunshine, and the shadows are all sorts of colours.

"What a big canvas!"

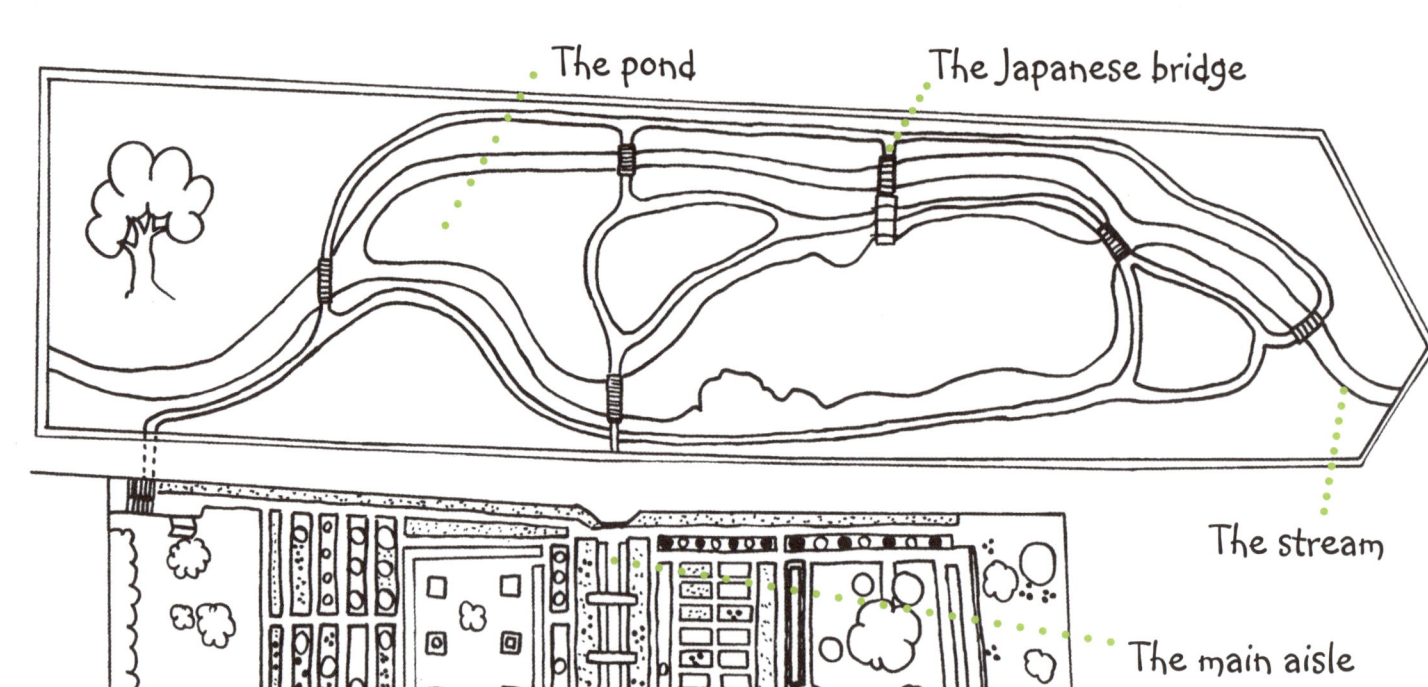

The pond
The Japanese bridge
The stream
The main aisle

What a view from up here! Colour in Monet's garden!

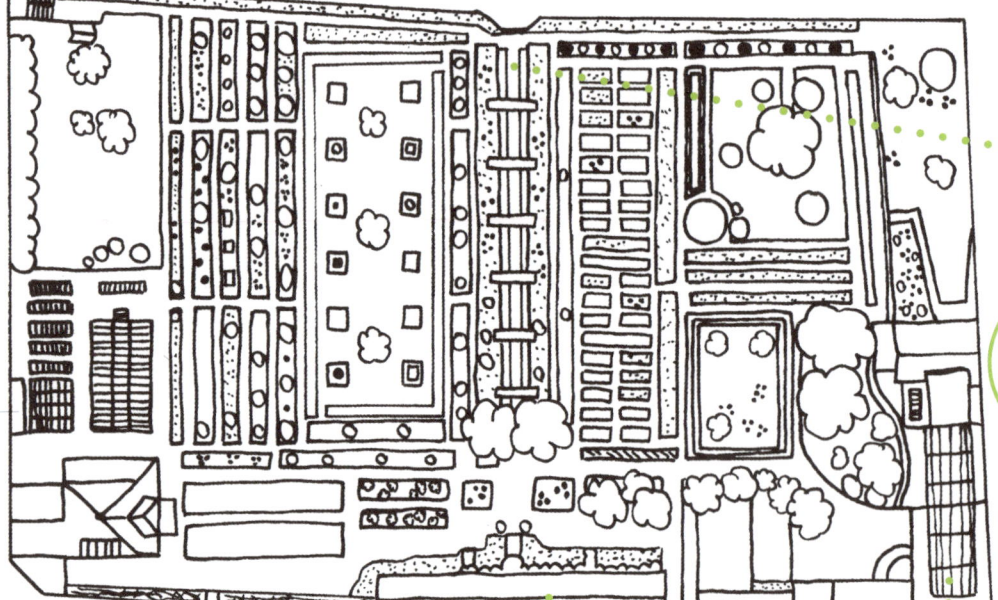

The house
The greenhouse

My painting is like my gardening.

The arches over the main path are covered with roses. The nasturtiums are splashes of orange on the ground. My garden looks like an impressionist picture!

The main aisle

Your turn to create the garden of your dreams! Use these flowers as inspiration to draw your own borders.

Claude Monet loves good food. In the blue-tiled kitchen, Marguerite the cook prepares lunch with produce from the vegetable garden. Monet has a large family and he likes to invite his friends for lunch.

Think up a menu with vegetables from the garden.

Starter

Main course

Dessert

Still, I hope he doesn't like snails with garlic!

Lunch is ready!

In the dining room, all the furniture is yellow. The room is decorated with the painter's collection of Japanese prints.

Monet's favourite dishes

Lightly-cooked asparagus.
Lobster and game, especially woodcock.
Lettuce, seasoned with pepper, a lot of olive oil and a little wine vinegar.

Colour in this pretty table, ready for the guests.

Monet creates a water garden, like a masterpiece. He has a large pond dug out and diverts a branch of the river Epte. The painter-gardener grows bamboo on a small island. The local farmers find it very worrying... They think that the foreign bamboo plants could poison the water and their cows. Monet reassures them.

Dragonflies, irises, water-lilies... The Japanese-style green bridge spans the pond. Purple wisteria twists around the bridge. Monet loves it here!
The calm and beauty inspire the impressionist painter.

Gardeners help him to tend the garden and the pond, so that the water-lilies are shown off at their best.

Look at my masterpiece!

It's siesta-time!

In the shade, little Jean is playing quietly by himself. What is he building? His dad paints him with affection.

Monet and his family have gone for a walk. Claude has set up his easel in a field full of poppies.

Camille shelters from the sun under her hat and parasol, while Jean picks a bunch of flowers for his mum.

Contemplation
A breeze is blowing on the hillside...

Mediation
The clouds are scurrying by, the grass is blowing in the wind...

"Fancy painting haystacks!"

Near his house, Monet rents some haystacks from his neighbour. He paints them over and over again, morning to night and in all types of weather. He paints more than 20 pictures!

20

In springtime, the garden is full of the scent of flowers. What beautiful colours!

Text: Catherine de Duve
Illustrations: Julie Dufour
Design: Véronique Lux
Translation: Rachel Cowler

PHOTOGRAPHIC CREDITS:
Claude Monet:
PARIS: Orsay Museum: *Woman in the garden*, c. 1867: cover, p. 14 – *The Luncheon*, 1873: cover, p.14 – *Water-Lilies, harmony in green*, 1899: cover, p.13 – *Monet's Garden, Irises*, 1900: p.2 – *In the "Norvégienne"*, 1887: p.12 – *Red poppies at Argenteuil*, 1873: p.17 – *Sketch of an outdoors subject: Woman under a parasols looking right*, 1886: p.18 – *Sketch of an outdoors subject: Woman under a parasols looking left*, 1886: p.19 – *Haystacks, end of summer, morning effect*, 1891: p.20
OTTERLO: Kröller-Müller Museum: *The Studio-Boat*, 1874: p.21
Private Collection: *Self-Portrait in Beret*, 1886: p.6
Shelburne: Shelburn Museum: *Wheels, snow effect*, 1891: p.20

Photos:
PARIS: Marmottan Monet Museum: *Claude Monet at Giverny*, 1921: p.2
Private Collection: p.3, p.6, pp.8-9, p.10, p.11 ©Kate'Art Editions

Visit our online shop

www.kateart.com